D1358690

PEOPLES *of the* SOUTH

SCN Media Center
P.O. Box 3000
Nazareth, KY 40048

SUNBIRD
PUBLISHING

First published 2001
2 4 6 8 10 9 7 5 3 1
Sunbird Publishing (Pty) Ltd
34 Sunset Avenue, Llandudno, Cape Town, South Africa
Registration number: 4850177827

Copyright © 2001 published edition: Sunbird Publishing
Copyright © 2001 text: Sue Derwent
Copyright © 2001 photographs: Roger and Pat de la Harpe, with the exception of the following:
D. Allen pp 4 (top right), 75 (top right), 82–84; Walter Knirr pp 7 (top left), 59, 75 (bottom left), 80, 81;
South African National Parks p 7 (top right & bottom); University of Pretoria pp 1, 6 (top), back cover.

Publisher Dick Wilkins
Editor Sean Fraser
Designer Mandy McKay
Production Manager Andrew de Kock

Reproduction by Unifoto (Pty) Ltd, Cape Town
Printed and bound by Tien Wah Press (Pte) Ltd, Singapore

All rights reserved. No part of this publication may be reproduced, stored in a retrieval system or
transmitted, in any form or by any means, electronic, mechanical, photocopying, recording or otherwise,
without the prior written permission of the copyright owner(s).

ISBN 0 62403 972 2

ACKNOWLEDGEMENTS

*The publisher, author and photographers would like to thank the following individuals
and institutions for their kind assistance in the compilation of this volume:
Dr Dai Herbert, Basotho Cultural Village, Botshabelo Historical Village, Kosi Bay Forest
Camp, Lesedi Cultural Village, Milimani Game Sanctuary, Shakaland, Shangana
Cultural Village, Simunye Zulu Lodge, Welkom Bushman Village, and the University
of Pretoria for help with photographs of artefacts from Mapungubwe.*

*TITLE PAGE This golden rhinoceros, found at Mapungubwe in the Limpopo Valley,
is an icon of wealth and status from an ancient royal burial ground circa 1000AD.
LEFT Prince Galenja is the great-grandson of Mkhosana Biyela, Shaka's cousin and a
prominent strategist in the military campaigns of the renowned leader of the Zulu nation.
OPPOSITE Ndebele murals are painted exclusively by the women, and allow them to
express their individuality in an otherwise strongly patriarchal society.*

Introducing the Peoples of the South

In a nation such as South Africa, where the population stands at about 44.6 million spread across nine provinces and speaking 11 different official languages – and an even greater number of localised dialects – it is little wonder that its peoples, with their various ethnic and cultural heritage, contribute enormously to the exciting diversity of this multicultural land.

By the time the first Europeans arrived on the southern tip of Africa, the area was already inhabited by an ancient culture, who today are considered the earliest indigenous people of South Africa. These were the KhoiSan, made up of the Khoi-Khoi and the San (or Bushmen). Although the beliefs and customs of these two groups were similar, there were differences that distinguished one group from the other: whereas the Khoi-Khoi were pastoralists who kept livestock, the San were purely hunter-gatherers.

The KhoiSan were already well established at the Cape when Dutch sailors first landed on its shores and had had a marked impact on the black peoples with whom they had come into contact. The languages spoken by the black peoples of southern Africa have, for example, been influenced by the KhoiSan. The

ABOVE *Until married or engaged, many young women – such as this Swazi maiden – in traditional areas go bare-breasted.*

Xhosa people, in particular, had an extended period of contact with the KhoiSan and their language remains peppered with click sounds they inherited from their early countrymen. The Bantu languages did not, however, change fundamentally over the last few centuries, and because of the similarity between them, historians have been able to piece together the speed and routes by which the Bantu people settled the subcontinent. The Bantu-speakers can generally be divided into two groups – the Nguni and the Sotho.

The precise reasons or events that triggered the great migrations of black people from Central Africa southwards about 2 000 years ago are not known, but it is accepted that many groups left their lands further north to seek new homes and pastures in the relatively unexplored territories that lay to the south. Those who settled in what is today known as South Africa are

ABOVE *It is customary for young Zulu men – and women – to don traditional dress for ancient customs and rituals such as weddings.*

descended from four major groups that are again divided into nine distinctive ethnic groups. The Sotho comprise the North Sotho, the South Sotho and the Tswana, while the Nguni consists of the Zulu, Xhosa, Swazi and Ndebele. The Shangaan-Tsonga – traditionally found in the Gazankulu and Mpumalanga regions – and the Venda people, who live largely in the Northern Province, fall in neither the Nguni nor Sotho groups, and each comprises a group of its own.

These migrant people probably arrived in the Limpopo River area in around 300AD. They were largely agriculturists, who grew crops and owned domesticated animals. Archaeologists believe that these groups moved down along the eastern coastal

ABOVE *In the often inaccessible rural areas of their mountainous homeland, the most convenient transport for BaSotho men is horseback.*

plain and then inland along the river valleys. Following these immigrants, waves of other groups continued to arrive in the southern regions until well into the 18th century. Although all these groups spoke Bantu languages, each had an identity of its own, with particular customs and traditions. And even within each group there are subgroups with similar or slightly different interpretations of customs and traditions.

With the movement of all these people, it is not surprising that there has been an interesting merging of lifestyles on a cultural level. For instance, there are two major groupings within the Ndebele: the Ndzundza and the Manala. The Ndzundza make up approximately 90 per cent of the Ndebele, and are now known as the Southern Ndebele. These Southern Ndebele settled in the Highveld areas to the northeast of what is today Pretoria, while the Manala or Northern Ndebele integrated with the Northern Sotho people with whom they enjoyed a close association.

The origins of the Ndebele remain elusive, but one of the most popular theories claims that they are an

ABOVE *Shangaan traditional healers encourage the presence of young children, considered symbols of innocence and integrity.*

ABOVE *Pedi women wear distinctive, brightly coloured, tasselled skirts as part of their traditional costume.*

offshoot of the Zulu people – although there is also some contention that their origins lie with the Xhosa. The Ndebele, together with the Zulu, Swazi and Xhosa, belong to the South Nguni-speaking ethnic group.

The Sotho can be divided into three broad groups: Northern, Southern and Western groups. The territory of the Southern Sotho is Lesotho and surrounds, while the Western Sotho are traditionally based in Botswana. The Northern Sotho are a heterogeneous group that includes a diversity of people such as the Pedi and the Lovedu. For years, the Lovedu, unlike the other predominantly patriarchal societies of southern Africa, have been ruled by a succession of legendary Rain Queens. Sotho societies, unlike the Nguni, who are structured around clans or family groups, focus on a totem, usually an animal – although, in other ways, they are indeed similar, particularly with regard to the structure of their lineage and extended families. Another example is the Tsonga people – once agriculturists and considered southern Africa's true fishermen – who were integrated with the Zulu to form a group now known collectively as the Shangaan.

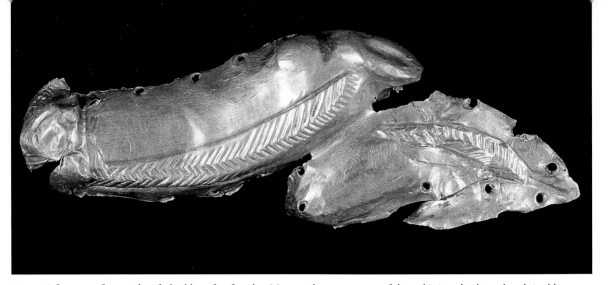

ABOVE *A fragment of an unidentified gold artefact found at Mapungubwe, a remnant of the sophisticated culture that thrived here.*

Although each of these groups has its own traditional home area, the black population of South Africa has spread throughout the country's towns and cities, and across its rural landscape. In many of the rural areas, customs and rituals are still part of day-to-day life and the cultures and lifestyles are still nurtured according to conventions established by the ancestors. At the same time, however, with the onslaught of modernism and Western culture, many traditions are being eroded by the demands of an increasingly industrialised and cosmopolitan society. Many beautiful and ancient customs and practices, once integral to traditional African culture, survive only as tourist attractions. Unless all the peoples of southern Africa honour the spirits of their ancestors and nurture their age-old conventions and wisdom, in time, they could be lost forever. It is fortunate, then, that archaeologists have discovered and been able to excavate a number of extremely important historical sites, such as those at Thulamela and Mapungubwe. Both provide considerable insight into the history of the people of southern Africa and cast some light on the people living in the region between 500 and 1 000 years ago.

Thulamela, meaning 'Place of Giving Birth', is situated on Thulamela Hill near Pafuri in the Kruger National Park, and radiocarbon dating indicates that it was inhabited from the 15th to the mid-17th century. While searching through the middens, researchers unearthed gold beads, charcoal, ostrich-shell beads, ornamental cowry shells, clay spindle whorls, and ivory and metal rings – proving that these people had strong links with the early traders off Africa's east coast.

ABOVE *Influenced by the colonialists, Basotho women began to mould clay display cabinets on the walls of their homesteads.*

ABOVE *The San people of the Kalahari painstakingly make beads from bones, quills and ostrich eggs.*

ABOVE Women in rural areas, such as these Venda, still wear traditional dress, but it is often influenced by Western styles.

excavations uncovered a royal cemetery of no fewer than 23 graves, three of which held golden rhinos and jewellery. Also discovered were carved wooden and ivory items. From these fine examples of work, it is clear that the original inhabitants of Mapungubwe were obviously skilled craftsmen, who produced characteristic pottery, beads, and ornaments of iron and figurines of both humans and domestic animals. Beautiful gold objects, such as the famed golden rhino, gold ornaments, sceptre and bowls were also found in the Mapungubwe graves, and show that the individuals who occupied this region were obviously not simply pastoralists and hunters – as early researchers have tended to portray them throughout history – but one of many early cultures that were indeed highly sophisticated.

ABOVE Gold excavated at Thulamela included gold beads that were probably part of royal armbands and necklaces.

Mapungubwe – which means 'Hill of the Jackal' – is another important archaeological site and is situated at the confluence of the Limpopo and Shashe rivers. This Iron Age African kingdom is thought to have existed between 700 and 1 000 (or even 1 300) years ago. Today, the hill is considered one of the richest archaeological sites in the whole of Africa.

Mapungubwe was an early Shona/Venda capital, but some researchers claim that it may have been the first capital of the ancient kingdom of Great Zimbabwe, as it echoes many of the features found in the later capitals of Great Zimbabwe – the most famous of which is the ruins of Great Zimbabwe in southeast Zimbabwe. What is left of Mapungubwe today points to previously unsuspected riches in the Cradle of Mankind.

Among the most important cultural treasures of Mapungubwe are some of the oldest gold objects ever to have been found in southern Africa. Early

ABOVE The stone walls of the royal enclosure on the Thulamela hilltop were reconstructed during the development of the site museum.

The San

The San, or Bushmen, are South Africa's earliest inhabitants and, although virtually extinct, are honoured the world over for their ancient and mysterious culture. The San once inhabited vast areas of the country, but today only remnants of their communities are confined to small areas of the harsh and inhospitable Kalahari sandveld regions of Botswana, Namibia and the Northern Cape.

Their early interactions with the migrating African and European settler communities irretrievably eroded their culture, and very little of their hunter-gatherer way of life has survived into the 21st century. During the 18th and 19th centuries, the diminutive San were regarded by both colonists and African tribesmen as inferior and large numbers were decimated. The population continued to decline steadily and today there are virtually no San living as they once had, roaming the vast African plains. The result is that the San communities of today are acutely aware of their heritage and are striving to preserve it.

BELOW The San leave little other than their footprints in the sandy desert as they travel.

ABOVE The San are skilled trackers, able to interpret and follow animal tracks through the desert for days.

Many old customs and beliefs remain intact, even though they have incorporated modern concepts into their day-to-day existence.

It is thought that the San's hunter-gatherer societies date back more than 10 000 years to the Later Stone Age. Evidence of this can be found in archaeological excavations in caves and rock shelters, as well as the rock paintings and engravings scattered throughout the country. Some of these extraordinary paintings, depicting scenes from everyday life, are thousands of years old, but the artists seem to have stopped producing their primitive art during the 19th century when colonial expansion was at its most aggressive.

There are literally hundreds of sites of rock art in all provinces of the country, but the area with the most prolific paintings is the Drakensberg range, considered to be one of the richest sites of rock art in the world, with approximately 600 sites and more than 22 000 individual paintings. A common theme of these remarkable works of art is human figures and animals – especially large antelope, such as the eland. Scholars have offered a variety of interpretations of the paintings and engravings, from the literal to the magical and mythological. The beautiful and delicate works provide some insight into the physical and spiritual lives of the early San, known throughout the colonial era and even in recent times rather disparagingly as Bushmen. Even though contemporary San communities no longer paint panels of rock face, many – and particularly the older generations – continue to nurture the age-old tradition of storytelling, their fascinating fables often embellished with music and dance as they are passed down from one generation to the next in the rich oral tradition.

The San people did not, however, form a single, large homogenous group. Nor did they comprise isolated groups. In fact, it was their apparent readiness to interact with other groups that contributed to their dwindling numbers and, over the centuries, they found themselves largely confined to the dry, hostile central regions of southern Africa such as the Kalahari, where they adapted their way of life to the environment from which they derive their sustenance.

The San have always been expert trackers and skilled hunters. Tracking herds of game is the job of men, but all the meat from a hunt is shared equally among the family group – although the man whose arrow first struck the beast is entitled to first choice. However, because hunting is dangerous and time-consuming, meat is not always the primary source of sustenance. The San meal may be supplemented by other items harvested from the wild, such as wild plants, berries, nuts, underground roots and bulbs, and honey. Water is a most precious resource in the arid conditions of the Kalahari, so food such as tsamma melons and juicy tubers and bulbs are vital to survival. Women collect these fruits and they are also shared among the family group.

BELOW The eland murals at Kamberg Nature Reserve are some of the country's finest remaining examples of San rock art.

San communities consist of a number of extended families who live and travel together. Each family is small and close-knit, but a member of a group is free to join another group at any time – a tradition occasionally utilised to diffuse disagreements. Groups travel from one place to another, following herds and gathering food, and the length of stay in any one place is generally determined by the availability of food and water. When there is not enough water in the pans and water holes of the desert, groups break up into smaller units, dispersing widely, and coming together again when the rains come or conditions improve.

Shelters are temporary structures built from a framework of branches covered in grass and scrub. Each family has its own hearth, which is the centre of the home and the gathering place for meals. A large central fire may be built for dances, ceremonies and other rituals. Music and dancing may form part of formalised rituals, but can also be spontaneous, such as celebrations to mark a successful hunt. Women usually gather in a group to one side, clapping rhythmically and singing, while the men dance around the communal fire, one behind the other in single file.

The San are widely recognised for their deep commitment to nature and the spirit. One of the ways in which they reflect this spiritual enlightenment is through the 'trance' or 'healing dance', which is reserved for men. The clapping of hands, stamping of feet, and rhythmic singing provides the necessary tempo to help the dancers slip into a state of trance, when the *shamans*, or healers, can contact the natural and supernatural spirits.

Animals are not merely a source of food, but also provide a wide range of raw materials needed for survival. Skins are traditionally prepared by men, and the leather is then used to make items such as small

ABOVE Animal engravings at Twyfelfontein, Namibia, are thought to have been made hundreds of years ago by the San.

carry bags, loin cloths, aprons, and skin cloaks known as *karosses*. The animals' bones are used to make the essential arrow shafts and tobacco pipes. Ostrich eggs often serve as containers for water and, once plugged, these vessels may be buried in the sand to be retrieved later when water is scarce.

The San are skilled craftsmen, making many of their decorative and functional items from products found in the wild. Tortoise shells and ostrich eggs provide the necessary materials for beads, bowls, 'snuff boxes' and other personal belongings.

When the men are not out hunting, much of their time is spent in the camp, discussing previous hunts and hunting strategies, and repairing their weapons. Their outstanding hunting skills can be related to their extensive knowledge of animal behaviour, and although religious beliefs may vary between groups, there are a number of common features, one of the most fundamental being that, in the beginning of creation, animals were people like themselves.

LEFT *Living in the extreme weather conditions of the Kgalagadi, the San people are a resilient folk.*

TOP *San gather to make the arrows that will facilitate the hunting of wild game.*

ABOVE *A small tortoise shell is a prized possession and may be used by the San for a number of purposes, such as to make beads or even use as a container.*

OPPOSITE *San women are skilled at gathering whatever useful plants and herbs they can find, while the men are traditionally the hunters.*

LEFT The human figures – hunting, in trance, as family groups – and depicted with animals need expert interpretation in order to understand more about the artists' spiritual heritage.

TOP The rock art of the Drakensberg is considered one of the richest collections of its kind.

ABOVE The San once ranged throughout southern Africa, as is evidenced by the spectacular rock art found in the Cedarberg Wilderness Area of the Western Cape.

OPPOSITE The eland, such as this beautifully depicted polychrome at Kamberg Nature Reserve, is thought to have played a significant part in the spiritual lives of the San.

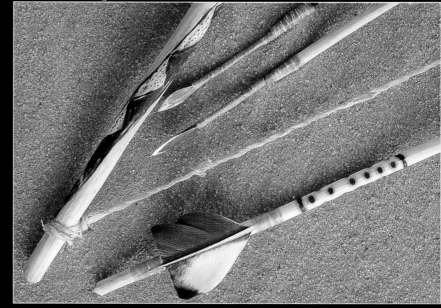

TOP LEFT San men prepare their arrows with skill and precision before a vital hunt.

LEFT Individual hunters have their preference of arrows, carefully fashioning their own arrowheads and shafts, which are usually made from bone.

ABOVE The weight and flight of an arrow can determine success or failure in the hunt for wild animals that will feed the family unit.

OPPOSITE San men hunt small antelope, hares and other wild game in the scrubby vegetation near the Kgalagadi Transfrontier National Park.

LEFT Even in the seemingly driest parts of the desert, San women find and dig up plants and roots, which they use for medicinal purposes.

TOP San communities consist of a number of extended families who live and travel together.

ABOVE All meat from a hunt is shared equally among the group, and because hunting is difficult, a carcass generally means an occasion to celebrate.

OPPOSITE The San are deeply committed to the spirit of the environment and are widely recognised for their ancient connections to the earth.

LEFT Ostrich shells, bones, animal horns and seeds may all be used by San women to craft beautiful necklaces and other useful items. Children are taught these skills at an early age.

TOP Decorated ostrich eggs are often used as a container for water, so precious in the desert.

ABOVE Every part of an animal carcass is utilised by the San. Larger horns make useful containers, and decorative patterns are burned into them.

OPPOSITE The San are patient and skilled craftsmen, making use of a variety of natural items for practical, ceremonial and fashion purposes, such as these striking necklaces.

ABOVE The rhythmical clapping, chanting and dancing of the women usually provide the tempo necessary for the male dancers to go into a trance.

RIGHT TOP Music and dance enhance the fireside fables – often recounting interactions between the wild animals of the region – for which the San are so well known.

RIGHT To celebrate a hunt or for more ceremonial occasions, the men dance around the communal fire in single file.

OPPOSITE In the ancient ways of their ancestors, the San continue to practise the skill of making fire by rubbing sticks together.

The Xhosa

The Xhosa, as with the Zulu, consist of a number of separate groupings such as the Pondo, Fengu, Cele and Xesibe – to name but a few – which today collectively make up the Xhosa-speaking people. Part of the Nguni group who migrated from northeast Africa, the Xhosa first settled in Zululand, and later, as a result of tribal conflict, moved south towards the Great Fish River, where they settled on the coastal plains and rolling hinterland of what is now the Eastern Cape. The area was inhabited by the KhoiSan and, following the interaction of these two groups, the Xhosa began integrating many of the KhoiSan traditions into their culture, most notably the clicks of the KhoiSan language that is today distinctive of spoken Xhosa.

Although affected by Zulu military expansion during the reign of Shaka, the Xhosa were not defeated. Nor were they defeated by the white settlers

Below *The Eastern Cape is the traditional home of the Xhosa people, many of whom still live in small thatched rondavels.*

arriving during the early 19th century. The Xhosa, however, did suffer terrible tragedy which, due to the prophecy of a young Xhosa women, Nongqawuse, contributed enormously to the downfall of the nation as an independent entity. Hailed as a visionary, Nongqawuse claimed she had had visions during which she was told that, on a certain day, the sun would rise blood red and at midday it would turn black, leaving the earth pitch black and destroying 'the unbelievers' (which included the settlers). Thereafter, there would be peace and plenty in the land. To facilitate this vision, the Xhosa were urged to kill their cattle and destroy their 'impure' crops. The prophecy, however, remained unfulfilled and, within 15 months, mass starvation decimated the population, leading to the demise of the Xhosa as a powerful nation.

The Xhosa traditionally built their *umuzi*, or homesteads, in a group that accommodated family units. Although modern trends are witnessing changes, the Xhosa remain a largely patriarchal society, with each household led by the husband, who is also the link between family members and external social or political structures. The head of the household is responsible for his family and women remain under his supervision – particularly an unmarried woman who, until she marries, remains subservient to her father, older brother or uncle in the event of her father's death. Once she marries, she falls under the male hierarchy of her husband's family. The position of the head of the household is hereditary and passes to the firstborn male, irrespective of his age, but this position has changed in many areas. With increasing Westernisation and the migrant labour system, many Xhosa households are today headed by women.

Above *Much like their ancestors, young Xhosa boys carry sticks while herding the family's cattle in the hills.*

Traditional Xhosa culture allows polygamy, but although this practice still takes place, the cost of securing a wife means that it is no longer as prevalent. The *lobola*, or 'bride price', is paid to the bride's father in livestock – often as many as 11 head of cattle – and these days a horse may be included in negotiations. Horses are a useful means of transport across the rough terrain in rural areas where many traditional Xhosa still reside. Cattle and children are not only a Xhosa man's pride and joy, but also symbolise his success and wealth. Cattle play a crucial part in the lives of the people – they are always corraled near the homestead – and are not only integral to marriage transactions, but also play pivotal roles in ceremonies and sacrifices.

ABOVE Oxen pull a handmade wooden sled used to transport bulk items such as thatching grass or firewood through the hills.

As part of the orderly transition through the stages of life, young Xhosa men and women are prepared for their roles in society by initiation schools. Many aspects of Xhosa initiation are handed down and adapted following early interactions with the KhoiSan. Still prevalent in modern times, young boys from traditional families must go through the *khwetha* or circumcision school or he will forever be regarded as a boy. There are many secret rites and ceremonies associated with *khwetha* initiation, and the process can take up to three months – although in modern times this is often shorter because many young men need to return to work. After a period of seclusion, young initiates smear their naked bodies with white clay and are covered in a single blanket or, in the old days, a sheepskin *kaross*. Contact with women is forbidden, and apart from the staple foods brought to them by children, the boys fend for themselves – usually by hunting. The boys live in simple grass huts, which towards the end of their initiation are set alight in a ritual symbolising the burning of their past. In this way, they leave behind their childhood and are accepted as men. In the past, initiates were expected to wait approximately four years after their *khwetha* ceremonies before they were permitted to take a wife.

As with the *khwetha*, many of the traditional rituals of the Xhosa involve strict adherence to codes of dress. Married women keep their heads covered, and hairstyles and headdresses – often indicating status –

remain fashionable. Women may wear magnificent turbans of wrapped cloth, with long beaded hair extensions and beaded rings. Headcloths of a variety of colours are twisted into attractive shapes and decorated with colourful headpins and beads. Depending on the area, a turban cloth worn well down over the eyes may indicate that the wearer has a child, but that she is still observing the ritual of respect she must show her husband's family. In the old days, a girl would go bare-breasted until she married, and a young woman of marriageable age may wear a headcloth and skirt, but no apron – only on marriage would she be permitted to cover her breasts. An apron of sheep or antelope skin signifies motherhood.

Older Xhosa women are often seen smoking elegant long pipes, beautifully decorated with beads, but traditionally, they were only allowed to smoke a pipe after they had given birth to a certain number of children. Men often carry their pipes and tobacco in a decorative bag. Snuff is taken using an elegant spoon, which was once made of bone, delicately carved and worn as part of a woman's headdress.

Many Xhosa people, as with many other people of African origin, still hold strong spiritual beliefs and follow traditional customs. The Xhosa believe that their ancestral spirits guide them through life, and they will appeal to their ancestors for assistance whenever major decisions need to be made. Most communication with the spirits is made through the mediation of a diviner or traditional healer. The Xhosa, with their long association with the KhoiSan people, are highly respected for their healing and divining abilities and as teachers in this field. Much like the Zulu and other traditional African societies, ordinary people may be 'called' to the profession through a dream or illness. Once an individual has

been called, a string – or strings – of white beads are bound around the right wrist, and the person is then counselled by a senior healer. White beads are important in this ritual because they symbolise purity, as well as guard against evil spirits. Practising healers are usually identifiable in Xhosa society by elaborately beaded headdresses decorated with goats' bladders, skins and charms. They wear crisscrossing bands of beads across their chests. Healers or diviners undergo an elaborate cleansing ceremony and slip into a trance before attempting to make contact with their ancestors.

ABOVE It is usually the older, married Xhosa women who smoke the long traditional pipes so distinctive of their culture.

ABOVE Xhosa men, traditionally the hunters, warriors and herdsmen, will also don the decorative beadwork finely crafted by the women for occasions of cultural significance.

ABOVE The Xhosa use a few different types of tobacco, mostly harvested from the wild.
OPPOSITE Dances may tell stories of battles, although costume styles may depend on the area.

PREVIOUS PAGE LEFT Beans are a staple food in many southern African cultures and it is the task of the women to sort them in preparation for the evening meal.

PREVIOUS PAGE RIGHT Young initiates, or *khwetha*, attending circumcision school smear themselves with white clay and wear no more than a blanket.

LEFT Sitting in the sun outside their huts, Xhosa women weave intricately patterned baskets from reeds and grasses harvested from the wild.

ABOVE In traditional Xhosa culture, girls participate in the domestic work of cooking, cleaning, fetching firewood and drawing water, from a young age.

OPPOSITE LEFT The colours chosen for the intricate beadwork necklaces often carry a symbolic as well as a fashionable message.

OPPOSITE RIGHT The traditional costumes of young Xhosa girls often imitate those of their elders for special occasions and cultural festivities.

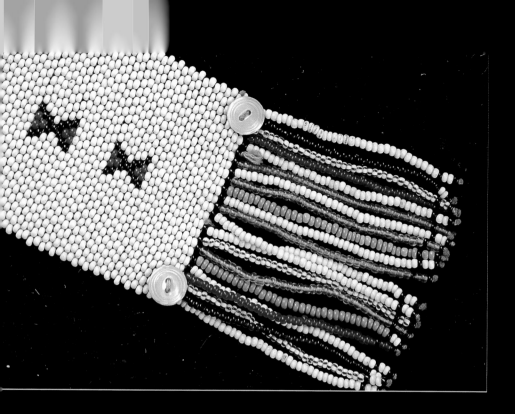

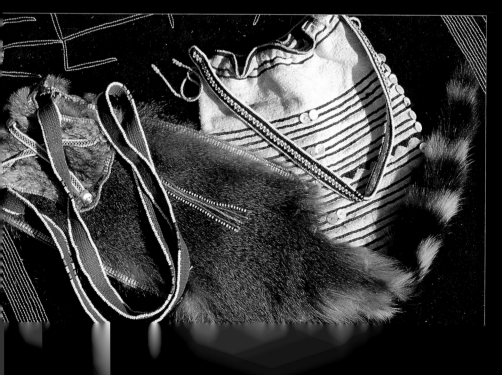

TOP LEFT Items of fashion, such as belts, today combine traditional and modern materials.

LEFT Tobacco pouches are made from delicately beaded animal skin or white cloth.

ABOVE Because smoking plays an important customary role in the lives of many traditional Xhosa, pipes and tobacco pouches are decorated with intricate beadwork.

OPPOSITE Gourds and horns covered in beautiful beadwork are used by traditional healers in which to store medicines or, by ordinary people, to carry charms.

OVERLEAF LEFT A traditional *sangoma* (or 'diviner') wears an elaborately beaded headdress to signify her status and role in the spiritual life of her community.

OVERLEAF RIGHT Linked by their ancestors to the Tekela-Nguni, the Pondo culture has many similarities to that of the Xhosa, most notably the decorative beadwork that continues to adorn both the body and items of cultural significance.

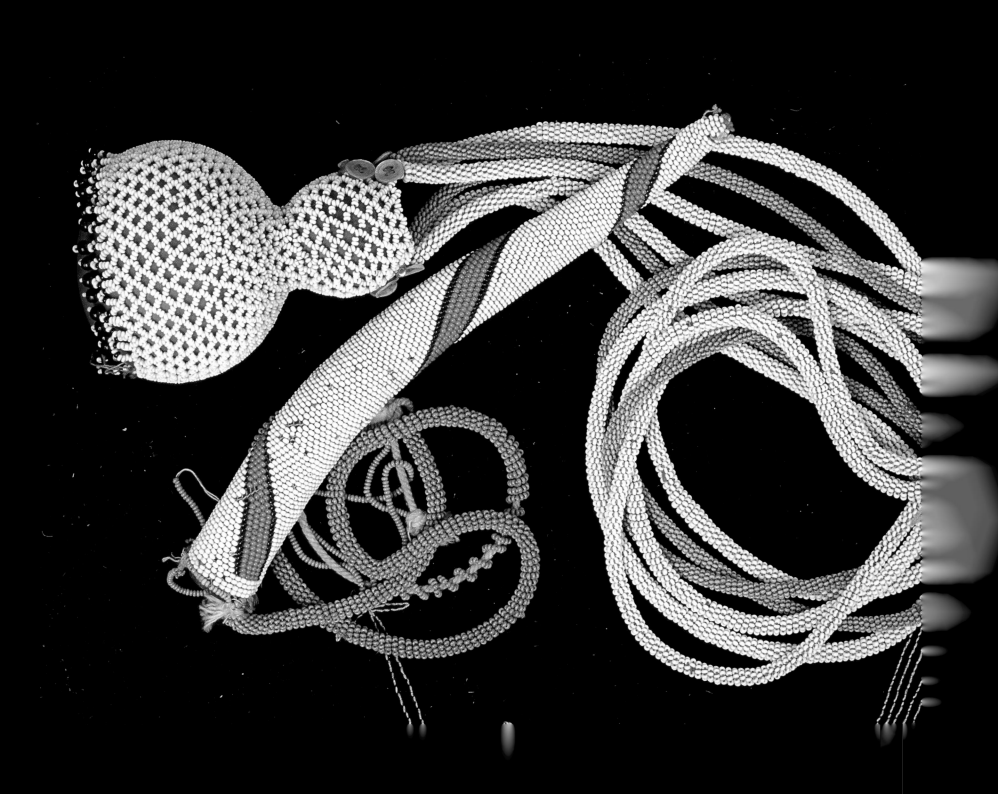

The Zulu

Before the 18th century, there was no separate Zulu kingdom and what is today considered the Zulu nation comprised a number of extended social units, many of whom paid allegiance to King Dingiswayo of the Mthethwa. It was only during the early 1800s that the Zulu began to emerge as a nation. Under the leadership and iron discipline of the great military strategist, Shaka, the Zulu nation increased in number from a scattering of insignificant villages to encompass other tribes and areas of the hinterland. Shaka's expansionist ambitions ignited a succession of skirmishes and an unprecedented movement of people throughout southern Africa, as people fleeing the Zulu warriors displaced other tribes in an attempt to escape the fighting.

Against this formidable background, many Zulu people still identify closely with their warrior ancestors, and many cultural practices, such as dance, still incorporate military conventions.

BELOW Wearing a brassiere at a wedding signifies that a woman is engaged or married, while maidens go bare-breasted.

A traditional Zulu *umuzi* consists of a cluster of dwellings that are home to a married man and his family. The circular homestead consists of a number of homes encircled by a high stockade, which would have prevented wild animals from attacking the occupants and their livestock. For hundreds of years, the Zulu lived in beehive-shaped houses: circular, domed structures constructed from saplings and grass.

A married man is the undisputed head of his household, and he may, even today, have two or more wives, depending on his personal wealth. Zulu families are generally close-knit units, with tasks divided along gender lines. Raising children has always been the responsibility of women, and women are also responsible for crops – but tending livestock remains the domain of rural men. Women prepare food, brew traditional Zulu beer, weave baskets and mats, and create items from beads, while men carve domestic items such as meat platters and serving spoons. In the past, many were spear and shield makers.

To the Zulu, cattle are more than simple beasts of burden, and Zulu men continue to put great store in their Nguni cattle. These cattle signify not only a man's wealth and status, but also his spiritual and mental wellbeing, and play a powerful role in traditional cultural practices. Without cattle, a man may not be able to pay *lobola*, and is thus unable to take a wife.

Many Zulu women are known for their pot-making skills as well as their talent for weaving. Traditional Zulu beer also plays a significant role in Zulu customs and most rural women still brew this beverage from maize or sorghum. Beadwork, too, is the terrain of women. Before glass beads became available in large

ABOVE There are over 100 different Nguni cattle colour patterns, each with its own distinctive name.

quantities during the 19th century, men and women wore strings of beads carved from wood, or crafted from seeds and berries, and threaded with a thorn onto the long sinews taken from the muscles in an ox's back. It is thought that the glass beads so strongly associated with the Zulu were originally made in Eastern Europe and Italy, and introduced to the Zulu by Portuguese traders and sailors.

Beads have always played an important part in the courtship rituals of young Zulus. Teenage girls often make small beaded squares called *themba* – meaning a combination of promise and hope or trust – which they give to young men with a colour-coded message woven into the design. Once a young woman has chosen her suitor, she may send him a necklace of white beads known as *ucu* to indicate her acceptance of him. In different parts of KwaZulu-Natal, different fashions have developed, with a variety of coloured beads and distinct patterns symbolising a wide range of meanings. These discrepancies have sometimes led to confusion and misrepresentation among scholars studying the beadwork. For instance, in some areas, green beads represent jealousy, while in another region, green may represent grass and carry the message, 'I will wait for you until I am as thin as a blade of grass.' In certain areas, yellow may also symbolise jealousy, while white most often represents goodness and purity, and blue signifies loneliness. If black beads are used, especially in the middle of a red square, this may mean that the girl does not love the young man, but may also be used to represent the black rafters of a roof, showing that the girl's love is as solid as the roof beams. But beads are not simply used for necklaces. They are also used to decorate domestic

ABOVE A young Zulu woman is expected to kneel in respect when she addresses an elder of her community.

utensils, headdresses and ceremonial sticks, and are interwoven with leather thongs and grass strips to fashion belts, skirts and aprons. These days, because of the expense of imported glass beads, they are being replaced by bright plastic beads that generally are much larger than the earlier beads – although they are still used for much the same functions.

The finest beadwork is displayed during traditional ceremonies, such as a young woman's coming of age, or a wedding, where festivities will probably include the great Zulu tradition of stick-fighting, dancing, singing and the drinking of Zulu beer. A Zulu wedding is more than a marriage between two people; it is the coming together of families, and an opportunity to air grievances. To other cultures, this may seem rather an awkward custom, but to Zulus, it is a good time to deal with potential problems that may later cause difficulties in the marriage. While any ceremony or festivity is an opportunity to dress in one's finest costumes, people today often wear a combination of both Western and traditional fashions. The traditional bride wears an ox-hide skirt – often inherited from her mother or grandmother – and a wide animal-skin collar, her face symbolically covered as a sign of respect. Only young, single women may go bare-breasted and without a head covering. Married women always have their heads covered, while those young women who are engaged to be married, will these days cover their heads with a hairnet and will often wear a store-bought bra in a modern version of keeping their breasts covered to indicate their status.

Long before colonists and missionaries introduced the concept of a Christian God to southeast Africa, the Zulus believed in a greater spiritual being, *Umvelinqangi* or *Nkulunkulu*. Humans could not approach this great being directly, and could only

BELOW A Zulu umuzi *(homestead), with its traditional beehive huts, nestles in the hills of KwaZulu-Natal.*

do so via their ancestors. Even today, when many ordinary Zulu people have even minor ailments or problems, they may appeal directly to their ancestors by undertaking a ritual sacrifice of a chicken or, if the problem is greater, a goat or even one of their cattle. This ritual is, however, usually presided over by a traditional healer who has the power to mediate between ordinary members of society and their ancestors. This gives many healers considerable influence in a traditional community. A trained *sangoma* is a diviner – usually a woman – who has been specifically 'called' and specially trained in the ancient methods of communicating with the ancestors. The *nyanga*, on the other hand, is a herbalist who is a master of medicine, with extensive knowledge of a vast range of herbs, plants, roots and even animal products that are used in the preparation of *umuthi*, or medicine.

Even though many Zulu people now live and work in urban centres, their belief in the power of their ancestral spirits may still run very deep indeed, and it is not uncommon for an educated, urban Zulu to consult a qualified doctor trained in Western medicine, as well as a traditional healer.

LEFT Many Zulu children and adults still enjoy a traditional game of *amagenda*, which involves throwing up small stones and catching them.

ABOVE A Zulu chief wears a leopard collar and headring, with cow tails hanging on his thighs, which indicate his elevated status among his community.

OPPOSITE Many Zulu women remain subservient, serving their husbands beer on their knees.

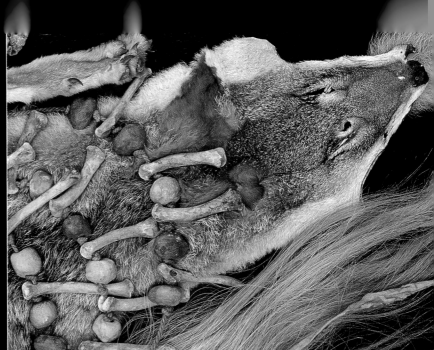

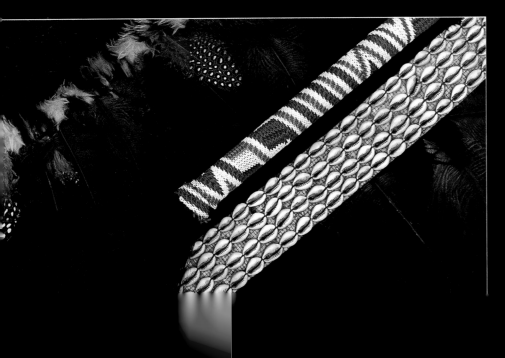

Previous page left It is unusual for Zulu women to wear leopard skin – even if it is synthetic – but this honour may occasionally be conferred on a young woman.

Previous page centre These days, larger, inexpensive plastic beads – rather than the old, smaller, imported glass beads – are often used in the crafting of the traditional jewellery worn by this young woman. The young Zulu man proudly wears a headband of animal pelt, which signifies that he is a man of some status in his community. Zulu men are some of the few in Africa who are not required to undergo the rites of circumcision.

Previous page right An elderly Zulu man fashions himself a *sagila*, or knobkerrie, which, according to custom, he will carry with him at all times.

Top left Wood carving, such as these spoons embellished with burnt patterns, is generally done by men in Zulu culture.

Left Among a *sangoma's* paraphernalia is a fly whisk and cowrie belt. Great secrecy surrounds these healers, but these items are believed to endow the *sangoma* with magical potency.

Above The *sangoma* will traditionally wear animal skins to cover the chest.

Opposite Many men make and decorate their own shields from carefully prepared cattle hide

LEFT A young woman will cover her face in the traditional manner of young Zulu brides.

TOP Young men prepare to take part in stick-fighting, a prominent event that forms a vital element of traditional Zulu weddings.

ABOVE The Zulu dance, usually depicting scenes from famous battles, is an integral part of Zulu custom and celebrations.

OPPOSITE It is usually Zulu women (left) who become *sangomas* or spiritual healers, while Zulu men (right) become *nyangas* or herbal specialists.

LEFT A young Zulu maiden shows off her *isicholo*, or headband, and her *mqhele*, or beaded necklace. Symbolic of her marital status and standing in the group, these items remain of considerable significance, even within relatively Westernised communities.

ABOVE AND OPPOSITE The traditional dress of these three young Zulu maidens consists of beaded headbands, legbands, necklaces and skirts. Like the unmarried women of so many other African groups, their breasts will remain uncovered until they are married.

LEFT The elaborately beaded headgear of the *sangoma* is unmistakable. The numerous loops that have been fashioned by the strings of beads are believed to welcome the spirits, who will sit on these tiny loops as they whisper into the ear of the diviner. Traditionally, the older and more senior Zulu women will also wear a heavy pleated skirt made by her husband from the hide of an ox.

ABOVE AND OPPOSITE Every traditional Zulu household uses clay pots for a variety of purposes, and these finely crafted containers are always made by women, often fired by packing dried aloe leaves around the pot, covering them with dried grass and setting it alight to bake them. Today, most traditional communities tend to use conventional plastic or enamel containers rather than handmade clay pots, so it is largely the ever-growing tourist trade that has contributed to the maintenance of skills such as pottery and weaving.

ABOVE The enormous *imiibiza* (beer pots) are usually set into the ground and are never moved. Beer is generally drunk from two types of pots, one larger than the other.

RIGHT The inside of an *nyanga's* hut is often hung with dried plants and herbs, bark and dried animals, all used for divining and interaction with the spirits of the ancestors.

OVERLEAF LEFT Teenage girls often make small beaded squares, called *themba*, which they give to young men with a colour-coded message woven into the design. *Themba* means a combination of promise, hope and trust, and designs and colours have specific connotations.

OVERLEAF BOTTOM LEFT Traditional Zulu weapons – including spears, assegais and knobkerries – may be decorated with intricate and colourful wirework.

OVERLEAF FAR RIGHT Clothing for toddlers and small children often consists of no more than a string of beads tied around the belly.

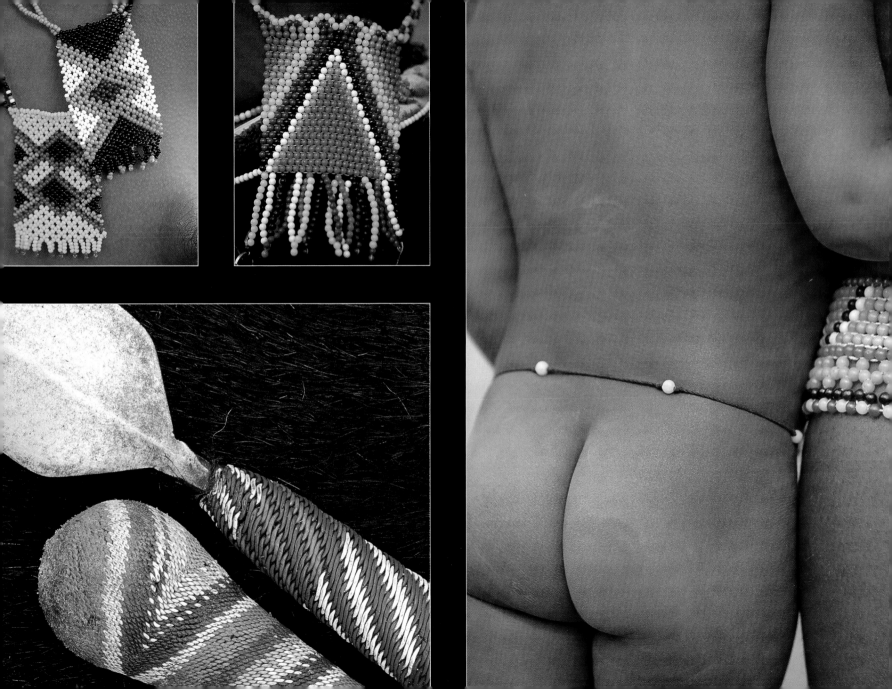

The Ndebele

The Ndebele are traditionally divided into southern and northern groups. The Southern Ndebele, or Ndzundza, as they were once known, is the group generally referred to as the Ndebele today. As a group, the Ndebele have been the subject of much interest and research, mainly because of their artistic nature, which has found expression and developed into an art culture of remarkable ingenuity and vitality. The Ndebele are perhaps most famous for their decorative beadwork, the large painted murals that cover the walls of traditional mud homesteads, and the striking traditional dress of the women.

As with many of Africa's indigenous people, Western civilisation is impacting on the Ndebele's unique lifestyle, on their distinctive clothing and their

BELOW *The bridged gateways of traditional Ndebele homesteads often have gabled features, which many historians think may have been influenced by Western architecture.*

unmistakable style of decorative visual art. However, rural women, with their typically creative dexterity, are adapting many of their traditional skills to more commercial applications in order to earn an income. In a few areas in Mpumalanga, traditional Ndebele villages have been established to encourage visitors to experience both the past and present cultural traditions of the Ndebele people. Many women still wear traditional ceremonial attire, children are dressed according to old custom and there are regular demonstrations of traditional house-painting techniques for which the Ndebele women are famous. But these tourist venues are not the only places where traditional Ndebele lifestyles may still be experienced. A drive through some of the rural Highveld in the northern provinces attests to the continuance of traditional customs, and even though Ndebele culture is currently in transition, many of the older customs are still practised – although often in a more contemporary and adapted form.

The artistic nature of the Ndebele is evident in nearly every aspect of their lives, from their clothing, ornaments and artefacts, to their building and home-decorating skills. In the past, homes were traditionally beehive-shaped structures made from saplings and thatch, but by the end of the 19th century the Ndebele were building rectangular dwellings and corrugated-iron roofing had largely replaced the thatch. There have also been some changes to the traditional layout of the homesteads. For instance, instead of being built in a circular fashion, the more modern homesteads are designed to face the front with the larger, main structure – usually the living quarters of the head of the household – situated in

ABOVE *Doorways, gateways and windows are important decorative elements of traditional Ndebele homesteads.*

the centre. Small, square windows are set on either side of a central door, which is usually shaded by an overhang or roof, leading out into a courtyard enclosed by a low mud wall. The interior of a modern Ndebele home is generally comfortable and practical. Benches are built around the perimeter of the room as a permanent part of the structure, and 'built-in' cupboards – remnants of the early settler influences, it is presumed – are made from mud-brick and plaster, smoothed down and hardened with cow dung before being decorated with the distinctive, intricate and colourful patterns associated with the Ndebele people.

Ndebele women take great pride in painting these murals, mainly onto the front walls of their houses, but also sometimes onto the interior walls. The precise origins of the mural painting are largely unknown, but it is thought that it emerged no sooner than around the middle of the 19th century when interactions between the Ndebele and their Sotho and Pedi neighbours led to the Ndebele building their houses with mud walls instead of grass. It was also at this point that the Ndebele began painting their walls – a practice originally learned from the Sotho.

Mural painting is done freehand, without a prior layout or design, and the most innovative and complex designs painted with the brightest colours are reserved for the front wall of the house. While the Ndebele artist is very aware of her environment, there are comparatively few examples of figurative decorations in the murals and stylised geometric shapes and designs predominate. Animals are seldom represented in murals, but if they are, they are likely to have been copied from a child's schoolbook. The artist seeks out graphic elements and incorporates these into her designs to symbolise the quality or characteristic of a particular object. The linear qualities of objects in the surrounding environment, such as telephone poles, car number plates and letters of the alphabet often provide a source of inspiration. Nowadays, many Ndebele women who work in cities have started incorporating urban imagery into the paintings on their rural dwellings, and details of churches, multi-storey buildings, stylised street lamps and electric bulbs may often be detected. Some Ndebele women explain that they may incorporate elements of modern life – such as electric lights – that they do not have, but may well aspire to.

There is no conclusive theory about how beads were introduced into Ndebele culture, and the types

BELOW *Wearing their traditional blankets, beads and body rings, these Ndebele women practise their age-old crafts.*

of beads have changed over the years. Beadwork has always been exclusively the work of Ndebele women and the symbolism encapsulated in hand-crafted pieces is often an expression of a woman's aspirations. For instance, abstract designs of houses are often incorporated into the beaded aprons they make for themselves and their daughters. Many older pieces of beadwork can be identified by the closely worked white beads that predominate, with only sparse geometric designs picked out in colour. Children are traditionally dressed in beaded goatskin aprons, and beaded *iphophi*, or dolls, are presented to young girls as fertility charms. The original Ndebele doll comprised a stack of small, beaded hoops, but commercial influences mean that they do not have the same symbolic value and the modern dolls are simply representational. However, the dolls are still used by traditional healers in certain rituals and they remain, of course, popular playthings for young Ndebele girls.

Although it is less common to see Ndebele men in traditional dress these days, many women still dress in traditional attire that reflects both their age and social status. Once a young Ndebele woman has completed her initiation, she is considered eligible for marriage. Prior to her wedding, a bride goes into seclusion for about two weeks, during which time she resides in a special structure erected within her parents' home. During her seclusion, she will make her own *liphotu* – a goatskin beaded apron representing the first stage of the wedding proceedings. Another apron, called the *ijogolo*, marks the culmination of the marriage process, which according to traditional Ndebele custom, actually only takes place after the birth of the first child. On her marriage, the bride will be presented with an *nguba*, a marriage blanket traditionally worn with the stripes running vertically,

ABOVE *The artistic nature of the Ndebele is evident in nearly every aspect of their lives, from clothing and craftwork to their beautiful homes painted with bright, geometric murals.*

and her husband will give her her brass or copper neckbands. Beadwork known as the *linga koba*, which means 'long tears', is proudly worn by the groom's mother and hangs down on the sides of her head. The beads are symbols of her joy at her son returning from initiation and his transition into manhood, as well as her sorrow at losing him.

A recently married woman will customarily cover her breasts by wearing a blanket over her shoulders, and around her neck she may wear a thick, heavily beaded hoop, known as an *isigolwani* or, sometimes, as *rholwani*. An *isigolwani* is made from huge, twisted hoops of grass, which are beaded and worn for adornment by initiated girls and married women in stacks around the arms and legs. The neck hoop indicates that, although the woman is married, her husband has not yet built her a house. But the copper and brass rings known as *dzilla* and worn around the neck have a far more powerful traditional meaning. *Dzilla* are worn only by married women; the rings are always given to the women by their husbands. Once the house has been built, the *rholwani* is cut off and replaced by *dzilla*. The more *dzilla* a woman displays, the wealthier her husband. In the past, it was believed that the wrath of the ancestors would be incurred should the *dzilla* ever be removed.

LEFT The thick, heavily beaded *isigolwani* are worn in stacks around the neck, arms and legs, and carry considerable cultural significance for the wearers.

ABOVE The copper and brass neck rings, called *dzilla*, convey a particular message about the wearer: these metal rings indicate that her husband has been able to provide a roof over her head and she is no longer required to wear the woven *isigolwani*, typical of initiate and recently married young women.

OPPOSITE Detail of the beaded apron, leg and ankle rings worn by married women.

ABOVE Ndebele beadwork contains many symbols, which are often expressions of the woman's personal aspirations and may symbolise events that have had some bearing on her life. Many of the patterns, designs and colours are, therefore, often associated with the domestic environment.

ABOVE Beadwork has always been done exclusively by the Ndebele women, who are renowned for their varied artistic skills. Their beadwork and creative mural paintings, which often contain similar symbols and designs, are an integral part of Ndebele culture.

LEFT Children are traditionally dressed in beaded goatskin aprons with just a few strings of beads on the head and crisscrossing the chest.

ABOVE The traditional beaded dolls that are today instantly recognisable as Ndebele artwork were originally presented to young girls as fertility charms, although in a slightly different form.

OPPOSITE *Sigolwani*, massive beaded rings, are worn in decorative stacks around the neck, arms and legs by both initiated girls and married Ndebele women.

OVERLEAF LEFT Innovative and complex designs, painted in the brightest colours, are reserved for the front wall of the house as it gives visitors their first impression of the family. Colour is used boldly and applied intricately, whether it be to a doorway, window frame or wall.

OVERLEAF RIGHT The clothes worn by Ndebele men are not nearly as distinctive as those of the women, and men seldom don traditional dress other than for special ceremonial occasions.

LEFT The original Ndebele doll was made up of piles of little hoops, but today, as a result of modern influences and commercialisation, it has become increasingly representational, and is usually made in a more Westernised form to make it more viable as a source of income.

BOTTOM LEFT Although few household implements carry the instantly recognisable designs and colours of the Ndebele murals, some, such as these home-made Ndebele clay pots, are decorated in their distinctive style.

ABOVE The art of weaving is largely dying out within the Ndebele community, although some women – particularly those in rural settlements who rely on their craftwork for income – still practise the art of weaving that has been passed down over the generations.

OPPOSITE Ndebele homes were once decorated with patterns executed by hand, using cow dung and charcoal.

The Sotho

The southern Sotho people, generally known as the BaSotho, take their name – meaning 'people of the dark brown river' – from the Caledon River, which runs along the base of the Malutis, the range that dominates their mountain kingdom of Lesotho. The Sotho settled on the central plains of South Africa and today still predominate in both Lesotho and across central South Africa. They were generally a peace-loving people who, headed by their famed leader King Moshoeshoe, remained undefeated despite clashes with European settlers and other indigenous groups. At various times during the expansionist reign of Shaka Zulu, the Sotho were displaced by groups fleeing Shaka's *impis* and they fled up into their mountain stronghold, now the independent Kingdom of Lesotho.

BELOW In the rocky terrain of mountainous Lesotho, horseback is the most practical means of travel for rural locals.

Traditional Sotho houses have changed from a rondavel-style hut with a low doorway, thatched roof and courtyard fenced off by a grass door, to a more conventional rectangular house, with roof, doors and glass windows typical of Western influences. Because of the cold climate of Lesotho, homes here tend to have thick walls and thick thatched roofs. Traditionally, these huts were built by men and women, using materials gathered from their immediate environment. The men would plant poles into the ground in a circle. Crossbar saplings or reeds would then be woven through the uprights and the walls clad in stone, to be 'plastered' over by the women with a mixture of mud and horse manure. Walls were also decorated by the women. Before the 18th century and the arrival of the missionaries and traders, wall decorations were generally finger-painted in simple but striking patterns. Later, women began to use forks to imprint the geometric designs on the walls of their homes, and used stones to impress patterns into the walls. Later still, as commercial paints became available, bright colours and other forms of modernisation were introduced. Men were responsible for thatching, and women would select, harvest and carry the bundles of grass to the homestead, where they would smear the walls and weave the door screens. After the 16th century, people started using small, tied grass bundles to cover the small window spaces and the traditional door, called a *tswahla*, was replaced with a sturdier version.

Influenced by European colonists, Sotho women also began constructing wall shelves as 'built-in cupboards'. This was a slow and painstaking process. Soil excavated by termites was ground up and mixed

ABOVE Intricately patterned blankets continue to hold much significance for even relatively Westernised BaSotho.

with horse manure which, because it is fibrous, gave strength to the structure. A small lip would be moulded into the surface of the wall and once this had dried and hardened, a further layer of 'plaster' would be added. Once satisfied with the construction, a final coat of cow manure was smoothed over the moulded surface, which was usually no wider than the length of a hand. As time went on, the women also began decorating their wall units with dots made from natural pigments, and later with more complex designs and commercial paints. Copying the style of European houses, the Sotho women would cut paper doilies or paper lace fringes to decorate the edges of their wall units, and display their plates and cups.

Traditional homesteads often had two fireplaces and two grindstones, one outside and one inside for days when the weather was unfavourable. Older dwellings had no specially constructed fireplace indoors, so people sat low on the ground to escape the smoke from the fire lit on the floor of the hut. In the 19th century, a special fireplace was built outside and consisted of low walls built in the shape of a cross, which provided shelter from the wind, no matter from which direction it blew.

One of the most important areas in a traditional Sotho household is the *kgotla*, a big open area used for meetings. Originally, only men were allowed to enter the *kgotla* and they would sit on stones, discussing matters of tribal and household importance, drinking and playing *marabaraba*, a traditional 'board' game. It was also in the *kgotla* that the old men would spend time with the youth, teaching and preparing them before they were sent away to initiation schools. The *kgotla* usually had three entrances, the main one through which the villagers could enter, another which was used by visitors, and a third, more secret entrance for the chief and his *indunas*, or headmen. Often, a *kgotla* would be below a conglomeration or hillock of large rocks, on which a sentinel would be posted to warn the villagers of approaching visitors. In fact, rocks are a particularly common feature of the Lesotho landscape, and made travel from one place to another difficult in the mountainous region in which the Sotho settled. Horses, therefore, played – and continue to play – an important role in the lives of the Sotho, and the sturdy BaSotho pony is much sought after.

Sotho people still true to the traditions of old may still be distinguished by the blankets they wear over their shoulders, as well as by the intricately woven

Below Clay oxen are made as toys by young BaSotho boys.

straw hats. Hat making is the art of the menfolk and there are generally three styles, although the coned hat with the interlocking grass arches – a symbolic depiction of the great Maluti Mountains of Lesotho – may only be worn by the *indunas* or royalty. One of the original hats favoured by BaSotho men was made from animal skin. Other hats take a more personal style and are woven from grass and worn day to day, or when working in the fields.

The traditional BaSotho blankets – a modern adaptation of traditional coverings of animal skins – remains, however, the most significant icon of Sotho culture. Today they are made in many colours and designs for everyday use, and may even be considered an item of fashion. The use of the blanket can be traced back to the 1800s when the BaSotho first came into contact with European missionaries and traders, and early versions were white, smeared with red ochre. In time, these were followed by 'five-and-a-half-feet-square' blankets of shoddy reused yarn taken from old woollen coats and clothing – until the BaSotho finally introduced the beautifully patterned blankets of the latter day. Many of the designs of modern blankets have remained unchanged for 50 to 80 years, or even longer. Whereas in Zulu culture, the newly married couple and their families receive woven grass sleeping mats, in Sotho culture, blankets play a significant part in the ceremonies. Although most traditional BaSotho wear blankets today, they once carried a stigma that indicated lowly status. This was about the time that missionaries, ever mindful of the heathen connotations of the old skin *kaross*, began to discourage people from wearing blankets. Also, as urbanisation of the Sotho population increased, blankets were associated with rural people who had refused to welcome 'progress'. However, during the

Above Women carry water from streams and springs in handmade clay pots balanced on their heads.

1980s, the status of the blanket took an upward swing, especially among BaSotho migrant workers. The migrants would not easily part with their blankets because, not only did blankets signify a unity and identification with the rest of the Sotho community, but the design of a blanket revealed much about individual identities: class, standing in the community, marital status and geographical origin. Even though many blankets are now worn simply for pleasure or as a fashion statement, the design and colour could – and still does in many rural parts – carry significance. The Poone, or maize design, implies fertility for men and women, and the cabbage leaf is a sign of prosperity. The blanket known as the Victoria is made from expensive wool, and indicates the wealth of the owner. The Seara Marena should only be worn by kings or *indunas*, and was originally made in England, while the Sefate is a well-known pattern based on the design of playing cards and includes a battle-axe. The manner in which a blanket is worn is also important. Stripes must always be worn vertically, because it is believed that horizontal stripes can stunt the growth, development and wealth of the wearer.

LEFT A design of the traditional BaSotho hat can indicate the status of a man. The hat with the intricately woven peak of the cone should be worn only by headmen or royalty.

ABOVE Playing a traditional board game is a favourite pastime for BaSotho men, and is one of the many traditional leisure activities handed down from one generation to the next, particularly among those BaSotho who continue to live in the rural landscape of Lesotho.

OPPOSITE LEFT AND RIGHT The shapes, designs and patterns characteristic of BaSotho hats and blankets are not only symbolic, but today also have functional and fashionable connotations.

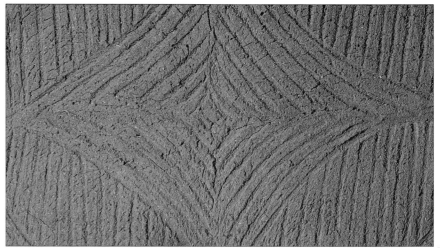

LEFT AND TOP Traditionally, Sotho huts were unpainted – patterns were impressed into the plaster.

ABOVE Mud-and-dung shelves are painstakingly moulded into the walls of the homesteads and richly decorated.

OPPOSITE A typical Sotho kraal, consisting of a number of mud-and-stone thatched rondavels, nestles at the foot of a sandstone ridge.

OVERLEAF LEFT AND RIGHT The elaborately patterned blankets pinned at the shoulder of BaSotho men are, typical of BaSotho design, often as colourful as the walls of the traditional homes.

LEFT Traditional beer is strained through a tightly woven basket made especially for the purpose.

TOP One of a woman's chores in many BaSotho households is to prepare the daily meal by crushing the staple maize on a grinding stone.

ABOVE The BaSotho tend to grow much of their own produce, such as pumpkins.

OPPOSITE Many rural families follow traditional lifetsyles devoid of modern conveniences.

LEFT A traditional BaSotho healer is unmistakable in his skin *kaross* and headdress, but it is his affiliation with the spirits that has earned him his status in the community.

TOP AND ABOVE Like many of their countrymen, BaSotho diviners consult bones, shells, coins and a variety of other objects collected from the countryside.

OPPOSITE BaSotho ponies are sure-footed beasts and an essential mode of transport in the mountainous terrain of Lesotho.

The Shangaan, Tsonga, Venda and Swazi

ABOVE Tsonga fishermen use rafia palm fronds to help fashion rafts, from which they check their distinctive fishing traps.

THE SHANGAAN

The grouping known today as the Shangaan is actually an amalgamation of Tsonga and Zulu people, who took their name from SoShangane, a leader of a Zulu *impi*, or military regiment, who had been sent to conquer the peaceful Tsonga.

BELOW The xitende*, a musical instrument expertly crafted by the Shangaan, produces a beautiful, haunting sound.*

The Tsonga had been scattered west of the Limpopo valley in Mozambique, and along the border of what is now the Kruger National Park. When the Zulu *impis* arrived, they found a peaceful agricultural society, where the land was fertile and there were plenty of cattle. Instead of herding the livestock back to Zululand, the warriors stayed and settled, and today the Shangaan people, speaking a variety of dialects, are found all over Mpumalanga, in southern Zimbabwe, and in Mozambique. They are still largely agriculturists, with groups following customs of both the original Tsonga people, as well as adapting and integrating many Zulu traditions into their culture.

Many Shangaan remain skilled agriculturists and farm maize, pumpkins, beans, *ntusumbulu* (a variety of potato and one of the main staples), groundnuts or peanuts. A wooden pestle and mortar is used to crush dried maize kernels into a powder, the main ingredient of a sticky porridge. While women plant and maintain their fields, men are required to prepare fields, and the whole family will help with the harvest.

With an apparently inherent love for music, the Shangaan have developed a number of musical instruments. The *fayi* – small, stubby wooden flute that produces a breathless, raspy, but haunting sound – is played by young boys, often when they are out herding cattle. Another Shangaan instrument is the *xitende*, a long, thin bow tied on each end by a taut leather thong – or, in modern times, wire – which runs across a gourd. This was a particularly popular instrument carried on long distances to alleviate the boredom of the journey.

THE TSONGA

For hundreds of years, the Tsonga people have harvested marine life along the beaches of Maputaland. Giant raffia palms, reeds growing around the numerous lakes and pans, and the dune forests have all provided resources on which the local Tsonga have depended for food, building materials and medicines.

The Tsonga remain highly regarded as skilled fishermen, and their fish kraals and trapping methods could date back to prehistoric times. The *fonya*, or fish drive, is one of their most fascinating traditions, and usually takes place during the winter months when many of the region's pans dry up. In the old days, when the water levels were low, the men would gather and, armed with spears and *fonya* baskets, head for the pans. A group would wade, waist-deep, into one end of the pan in a long row, and 'beat' the water, driving fish across the pan. When a shoal was isolated, the men would trap the fish in baskets. The hole at the top of the basket allowed them to grab or stab the fish with a spear. These days, the demand for migrant labour means a shortage of men in rural areas, and it is generally the women who organise the fish drive.

Almost sculptural in their simple beauty, the Tsonga fish kraals, or traps, are built in the clear waters of Kosi Bay and consist of a fence of thin poles woven with reeds, carefully placed in the waterways in such a way that fish entering from the sea or leaving the lake are guided into the circular kraal and trapped there. The local fisherfolk check their traps at particular times of the day and spear the fish caught inside.

There are very few 'new' fish kraals, as most have been handed down or maintained by a single family for generations. Most are still in use on a daily basis.

THE VENDA

Like many other indigenous groups, the Venda – found largely in the Northern Province, and well known for their skilled traditional healers and ancient spiritual beliefs – hold particular places sacred.

Near Nzhelele, between Thohoyandou and Makhado, are the sacred Phiphidi Falls and the enchanted Guvhukuvhe Pool. The locals consider

BELOW The sacred pool at the foot of the Phiphidi falls holds considerable significance for the local Venda people.

the falls and the pool below to be home to *Zwidutwane*, the water spirits, and often leave offerings of food, flowers, and other gifts on the rocks around the pool.

Forests are often proclaimed sacred, usually when they are the burial sites of chiefs. According to Venda legend, the sacred Lake Funduzi in the Thathe Vondo Forest is the home of a white crocodile, and parts of the forest are haunted and protected by white lions. The forest was originally settled by medicine men and used for ritual sacrifice and is thus enveloped in superstition. As a result, nobody is permitted to walk in those areas and, because the lake is believed to be the home of the god of fertility – a sacred python who made his home here – no one washes or swims in these waters. Legend also has it that when the wife of the god realised that her husband was a python, she ran away. This brought about a dreadful drought during which the people suffered terribly.

The traditional and now famous Domba (or Fertility) Dance is a relic of the dance that was originally performed by young Venda virgins to appease the god in the hope that he would send the rains. To this day, offerings are still made every year by the local people to secure good rains for the region. Young, bare-breasted women dance the Domba – now also known as the Python Dance – way into the night in a slow rhythmic line, weaving to and fro to the ancient beat of African drums.

THE SWAZI

Although up to 40 per cent of Swazis now reside in South Africa, the traditional home of the Swazi nation is Swaziland. The people living in the small land-locked kingdom are closely related, through their Nguni origins, to both the Zulu and Xhosa, and much of their culture is linked inextricably to those of their

ABOVE Swazi maidens dress in full traditional regalia for the Reed Dance, a contemporary variation on the ancient custom.

nearest neighbours, the Zulu. The Swazi, like the Zulu, are traditionally pastoralists who place enormous importance on their cattle. Another shared tradition is that of the Reed Dance, which takes place annually at the beginning of spring. The Reed Dance is also a dance of the virgins, at which, according to tradition, the Swazi king chooses one of the maidens to become his new wife. These days, the occasion is also used to promote chastity among teenagers. Hundreds of bare-breasted young women, adorned with colourful traditional beadwork and carrying long canes, swing and sing in rows before the assembled audience from all the Swazi clans, who gather to celebrate this tradition. It is also an occasion for the traditional Swazi regiments to show off their dancing skills.

ABOVE A Tsonga diviner 'throws the bones' from a specially woven container onto a grass mat outside her home.

ABOVE Tsonga boys collect water lily buds, a great delicacy, from shallow pans in Maputaland.
OPPOSITE The ancient Tsonga fish traps of Kosi Bay each belong to a different family.

TOP LEFT The traditional Tsonga fisherman, responsible for the upkeep of his family traps, will clear the traps using a spear specially crafted for this purpose.

LEFT Tsonga men are also expert weavers, and fashion not only their fish traps, but also hats and other handiwork from the fronds of indigenous palms.

ABOVE Repairing and maintaining the ever-important fish traps by weaving short strong sticks and palm fronds, is an on-going process necessary for survival.

OPPOSITE The *fonya* fish drive requires the use of traditional woven baskets and, apart from its significance for the local fishing community, the event is also a popular tourist attraction for the region.

ABOVE AND OPPOSITE In the dark of the night, as the drums pound, young Venda maidens weave rhythmically around in single file and perfect synchronicity at the annual performance of the Domba Dance. This fertility dance is traditionally performed by virgins in order to appease angry gods so that they will send rain.

LEFT A bare-breasted young Swazi maiden will don all her finery for the famed Reed Dance, an age-old custom in which marriageable young women gather at the Queen Mother's home, from where they are sent off to harvest reeds in order to build a windbreak. The sixth and seventh days of this ritual are celebrated with song and dance.

TOP Swazi king Mswati III is accompanied by his headmen as he arrives for the annual Reed Dance, at which he would traditionally be expected to select a new wife.

ABOVE, OPPOSITE AND OVERLEAF Hundreds of young Swazi maidens, carrying their freshly harvested reeds, take part in the exciting and colourful annual festival of the Reed Dance.

SCN Media Center
P.O. Box 3000
Nazareth, KY 40048